THINGS YOU SHOULDN'T SAY PAST MIDNIGHT

Peter Ackerman

BROADWAY PLAY PUBLISHING INC
224 E 62nd St, NY, NY 10065
www.broadwayplaypub.com
info@broadwayplaypub.com

THINGS YOU SHOULDN'T SAY PAST MIDNIGHT
© Copyright 2000 by Peter Ackerman

Book design: Marie Donovan
Page make-up: Adobe Indesign
Original cpy editing: Michele Travis
Typeface: Palatino

THINGS YOU SHOULDN'T SAY PAST MIDNIGHT opened at the Promenade Theater, New York City, in May 1999. The producers were Good Friends L L C— Jeffrey Richards/Michael Rothfeld, Jean Donamnian, Ted Snowden, Steven M Levy, and Leonard Soloway. The cast and creative contributors were:

NANCY.. Erin Dilly
BEN ....Mark Kassen
GRACE... Clea Lewis
GENE...Jeffrey Donovan
MARK... Andrew Benator
MR ABRAMSON .... Nicholas Kepros

Director..John Rando
Set design...Rob Odorisio
Costume design...Tom Broecker
Lighting design...Donald Holder
Sound design... Peter J Fitzgerald
Casting... Jay Binder
Production stage manager .... Karen Moore
Technical supervisor .... Rob Conover

CHARACTERS & SETTING

NANCY
BEN
GRACE
GENE
MARK
MR ABRAMSON

Time: October

Place: New York City

With thanks to Jeffrey Richards

Scene One

(Two A M. Bed downstage center. NANCY *on her back, head downstage.* BEN *in* NANCY, *his hands flat on the mattress. Sex rising to climax.)*

NANCY: Ohh…yeah…

BEN: Ohh…

NANCY: Ohh…Yeah…

BEN: Ohh…

NANCY: Aah…yeah…

BEN: Ohh…

NANCY: Aaahh…aaahh…

BEN: Ohh…

NANCY: Yeah…yeah…

BEN: Ohh…

NANCY: …ohhh…aah…

BEN: Ohh…

NANCY: Yeah…yeah…

BEN: Ohh…

NANCY: Aah…ohhh…

BEN: Yeah…

NANCY: Yes, Yes.

BEN: Ohh…

NANCY: Yes, Yes!

BEN: Ohh…

NANCY: Yes! Do me!!

BEN: Ohh…

NANCY: Do Me! YES!

BEN: Ohh…

NANCY: YES! Do Me!!

BEN: Ohh…

NANCY: DO ME! DO ME!

BEN: OHH…

NANCY: YES! DO ME!!

BEN: OHH…

NANCY: DO ME DO ME DO ME!!!!

BEN: Ohh…

NANCY: DO ME DO ME DO ME!!!!!

BEN: Ohh…

NANCY: *(Climaxing)* DO ME! DO ME!! DO ME!! DO ME!!! DO ME!!!! DO ME YOU HOOK-NOSED JEW!!!!!

(Pause)

BEN: What?

NANCY: Hmm…

BEN: What?

NANCY: Hmm…

BEN: What did you say?

NANCY: Hahhh…

BEN: Excuse me. What did you just say?

NANCY: When?

BEN: Just now.

NANCY: I don't know.

BEN: You said something.

NANCY: Did I?

BEN: Yes.

NANCY: What?

BEN: I don't know. That's what I'm asking you.

NANCY: Oh, that felt nice!

BEN: *(Persistent)* What did you say?

NANCY: *(Still in the sex)* That felt good!

BEN: Would you answer my question!

NANCY: What?

BEN: You said something just now when you came.

NANCY: What did I say?

BEN: I don't know! You tell me!

NANCY: "Do me?"

BEN: After that.

NANCY: What?

BEN: That's what I'm trying to find out!

NANCY: I think I said "do me" after I said "do me."

BEN: After all the "do me's" you said something else.

NANCY: I just said "do me".

BEN: At the end.

NANCY: "Me!"

BEN: The very end.

NANCY: I screamed "Me!"

BEN: You screamed something else.

NANCY: "I love you!"

BEN: That's not what you screamed.

NANCY: But I do.

BEN: Would you tell me what you screamed.

NANCY: I don't know.

BEN: You called me something.

NANCY: Lover.

BEN: No.

NANCY: Baby.

BEN: No.

NANCY: Sweetpea?

BEN: You called me a name.

NANCY: Was it mean?

BEN: Yes it was mean.

NANCY: You know I like to talk mean. It's sexy.

BEN: To a degree.

NANCY: So what's the problem?

BEN: You really don't remember what you called me?

NANCY: No!

BEN: I think you said…

NANCY: I was ecstatic.

BEN: I'm pretty sure…

NANCY: I was coming!

BEN: You called me a hook-nosed Jew. (Pause) You called me a hook-nosed Jew.

NANCY: That's crazy.

BEN: I know.

NANCY: I did not.

BEN: Yes you did.

NANCY: There is no way I said that.

BEN: I heard you.

NANCY: Were you coming?

BEN: Yes. But I stopped.

NANCY: You didn't come?

BEN: That's not the point!

NANCY: You can go crazy if you don't come.

BEN: I'm not the point! You are the point! You called me a hook-nosed Jew.

NANCY: *(Pause)* Jesus Christ. *(Pause)* Jesus Fucking Christ.

BEN: It's rather surprising.

NANCY: Are you sure I said that?

BEN: Well, I'm not creative enough to make it up.

NANCY: Wow.

BEN: Right.

NANCY: I don't know what I was thinking.

BEN: I'm sort of wondering that myself.

NANCY: I mean, I really don't know.

BEN: Do you have a problem?

NANCY: With what?

BEN: My Jewishness?

NANCY: Your...? No! Oh God, no! I mean... No!

BEN: You mean what?

NANCY: I mean nothing.

BEN: You said "I mean." What do you mean?

NANCY: I've never dated a Jewish guy before.

BEN: Okay. So there is a problem.

NANCY: It's not a problem. It's just...

BEN: What?

NANCY: Maybe subconsciously…it seemed dirty.

BEN: Dirty?

NANCY: Yeah. Dirty, sexy, nasty. I like nasty sex.

BEN: So you called me a hook-nosed Jew?

NANCY: In a sexy way.

BEN: You racially slurred me!

NANCY: I wonder what I meant.

BEN: You're not the only one.

NANCY: I mean, it's okay to get nasty, but maybe racial epithets are bad.

BEN: Does it bother you that I'm Jewish?

NANCY: No. I told you. I don't even think about it. *(Beat)* I don't even know what it means.

BEN: You don't know what what means?

NANCY: You don't seem any different from me.

BEN: But apparently you have feelings about it.

NANCY: Good feelings. Like you're responsible, and family-focused, and great with money.

BEN: Uh huh.

NANCY: That is what they say that about Jewish guys, you know. They're sensitive and good Dads. They're not gonna blow your brains out. That's a legitimate concern. You don't know people. I'm glad you're Jewish. I mean, not that I think about it. You seem just like me.

BEN: But apparently you…

NANCY: Except your nose.

BEN: My nose?

NANCY: Yeah. You know. Your nose.

BEN: What about my nose?

NANCY: You have a Jewish nose.

BEN: Uh huh.

NANCY: So you look Jewish.

BEN: I am Jewish.

NANCY: I know. That's what I'm saying.

BEN: Then you feel...

NANCY: I love your nose!

BEN: Fine.

NANCY: It's strong.

BEN: Fine.

NANCY: Like a beak!

BEN: Oh. That's terrific.

NANCY: *(Seeing him)* And the rest of your face, it's...

BEN: What?

NANCY: It's Jewish. You definitely look Jewish.

BEN: I am Jewish!

NANCY: I know you are. Stop saying that.

BEN: You keep bringing it up.

NANCY: It could just be your nose.

BEN: Nancy...

NANCY: It is weird that you're Jewish.

BEN: Why?

NANCY: I'm from Grant's Pass. We don't have Jews out there.

BEN: So you do think about it.

NANCY: Maybe it's like black people calling each other nigger.

BEN: But you're not Jewish.

NANCY: So?

BEN: So would you scream "Do me, you nigger" to a black guy?

NANCY: Well…if I was coming.

BEN: I don't think so.

NANCY: When I come I like to get to the core. You know? I like to say what I never get to say. 'Cause you get to get inside me, but I never get to get inside you.

BEN: So you called me a hook-nosed Jew?

NANCY: So I call you whatever I'm not allowed to call you! It's exciting. It feels good to say "Do me you hook-nosed Jew!" What do you do when you're just with Jewish people?

BEN: We eat bagels.

NANCY: When you're with your family. I've never even met your family, and we've been dating six months.

BEN: It's a long way to Chicago.

NANCY: But they came here. They met your dissertation advisor. Hey, wait a minute. He's Jewish, isn't he? Doctor Kornstein. *(Pronounces it "Stine")*

BEN: Stein. *(Pronounces it "Steen")*

NANCY: Steen. That's a Jewish name, right? Do you only introduce them to Jewish people?

BEN: Yes. I only introduce them to Jewish people. In fact, they've never met a non-Jew. I had to show them pictures in a book.

NANCY: Why would they meet your dissertation advisor and not your girlfriend? I am your girlfriend, aren't I?

BEN: Yes. Of course you are.

NANCY: Then why don't you ever tell me about the Jewish stuff?

BEN: Because there's nothing to tell.

NANCY: What's it like in synogogue?

BEN: Oi yoi yoi...

NANCY: You see that? "Oi yoi yoi." What's that?

BEN: Oh Nancy.

NANCY: No, really. It's like a cult. Tell me what you do in synogogue.

BEN: I don't know.

NANCY: You can tell me, Ben. I'm your girlfriend, remember?

BEN: That's the second time you've said that.

NANCY: I like saying it.

BEN: I like when you say it too.

(BEN *and* NANCY *look at each other.*)

NANCY: Tell me about the prayers.

BEN: *(Taking box of Chinese food)* They're just prayers, you know? We say the same thing we've been saying for thousands of years, and it's communal, so it feels good. It's not that complicated.

NANCY: Do you believe in God?

BEN: Nancy. It's not an easy question, "Do you believe in God." We could say "God" and mean two different things.

NANCY: Tell me what you mean.

BEN: It's not that simple. Brilliant people spend lifetimes, they write volumes trying to answer that question.

NANCY: So tell me volumes. You're smart. You have a PhD.

BEN: Not in Theology. In English. And I don't even have it yet. I can barely tell you what a 19th Century poet says.

NANCY: Tell me what you say.

BEN: I don't know.

NANCY: Well try.

BEN: Well... Yes. I suppose I feel some force beyond you and me.

NANCY: You have faith.

BEN: Yes. I have faith.

NANCY: So you believe in God.

BEN: Yes. I believe in God.

NANCY: I believe in God too.

BEN: Great. Let's throw a party.

NANCY: Why are you making this so difficult?

BEN: Nancy! We were having sex, and you called me a hook-nosed Jew! Do you have any clue how bizarre that is? Do you know how many times I have been called a hook-nosed Jew in my life?

NANCY: How many?

BEN: Guess.

NANCY: Five?

BEN: No.

NANCY: Ten?

BEN: Nancy! No! None! Zero! No one has ever called me a hook-nosed Jew in my entire life. I am the least persecuted Jew in the universe. I am Mister Assimilation. You might as well call me Chip.

NANCY: You're getting snide.

BEN: Well it's offensive. I'm a little rattled.

NANCY: That's why we have to work it out.

BEN: I want to work it out, but you can't assume I won't be rattled.

NANCY: I know you're rattled. That's why I want to talk to you.

BEN: Okay. Fine. I want to talk to you too, but I'm rattled. *(Handing her food)* Here. Take this. It's disgusting.

NANCY: What is it?

BEN: Eggplant with rotten fungus. Uchhh. *(He rises to dispose his box in a garbage can.)*

NANCY: The fact that we're on new ground means that we have to talk about new things, and all I'm getting at is that maybe sex is a way to experience God.

BEN: That's what you're getting at?

NANCY: Yes. Don't you think we sometimes have divine sex?

BEN: Yes.

NANCY: So maybe in general I believe you experience God more through sex and through people than through prayer.

BEN: In some twisted kind of way, that's actually very Jewish.

NANCY: Is it?

BEN: Yes. Minus the sex. But we do have to pray communally. We confess our sins communally. Martin Buber says you find God in every person and every object that you encounter if you engage in its divinity.

NANCY: Well that's what I believe.

BEN: Fine.

NANCY: So maybe I'm Jewish.

BEN: I don't think so.

NANCY: Why not?

BEN: Because you look like Maria Von Trapp.

NANCY: Well maybe everyone in my family converted.

BEN: Okay, fine, you're Jewish.

NANCY: Then I could call you a hook-nosed Jew.

BEN: Aah...maybe. If you were joking.

NANCY: I was joking.

BEN: You were coming.

NANCY: Well I believe you find God in people even when they're sinful.

BEN: So you called me that for the pleasure of sin?

NANCY: Yes.

BEN: I see. Well that's very interesting, but I think sex does more than just lead to God, okay? I think it also reveals people.

NANCY: What does that mean? I hate Jews?

BEN: It means we're different, and talking won't make us more alike than we are.

NANCY: Ben!

BEN: What?

NANCY: Don't be that way. I'm trying to bridge the gap.

BEN: The gap it seems is wider than I thought. It's not even a gap. It's more like a canyon...

NANCY: It's a fissure.

BEN: It's a fucking earthquake.

NANCY: I don't think so.

BEN: Listen to me. The whole point of being in love is that you don't have to spend all your time bridging the gap. You know? The other person just gets it.

NANCY: Well that's crap, Ben. Everyone has to bridge the gap, no one just gets it, and sometimes you make mistakes, okay? Especially the people closest to you. Sometimes even your mother makes mistakes.

BEN: My mother has never called me a hook-nosed Jew.

NANCY: Ben!

BEN: What?

NANCY: *(Gathers herself)* When you're with someone everyday, you see more than just who the person is. You see what passes through her.

BEN: And this passed through you.

NANCY: Everything passes through everybody. Haven't you come and said "Rape me?" Huh?

(BEN is silent.)

NANCY: That's pretty weird.

BEN: That's different.

NANCY: You're a guy. You shouldn't say "rape me." I think that's weird.

BEN: It is not!

NANCY: I think a woman saying "rape me" is weird.

BEN: At least I don't say "Rape me, you White Trash Hillbilly!"

NANCY: BEN!

BEN: I'm sorry.

NANCY: Is that what you think of me?

BEN: No. Of course not. I was showing you what it feels like. It's not so nice is it?

NANCY: I think it's bad enough you say "rape me!" That implies I'm a rapist. You think I like that?

BEN: You do like it!

NANCY: Well...yes, I happen to like it. But that's not the point. The point is I don't like you calling me a rapist, let alone a White Trash Hillbilly.

BEN: The point is you admitted that you like it when I say "Rape me!"

NANCY: So?

BEN: So you can't make up things I might say that you might not like. You actually called me something I don't like.

NANCY: So tell me.

BEN: I am telling you!

NANCY: Good.

BEN: In the heart of every Jew is the fear of what you said.

NANCY: Good.

BEN: Why do you think I go out with you? I don't want to be Jewish!

(Pause)

NANCY: Whoa...

BEN: I didn't say that.

NANCY: Whoa...

BEN: I didn't mean it.

NANCY: Then why did you say it?

BEN: I didn't.

NANCY: Yes you did.

BEN: Well it doesn't matter, 'cause I don't feel it.

NANCY: You did when you said it.

BEN: No I didn't. You provoked me!

NANCY: Provocation reveals people.

BEN: Not at three in the morning. Provocation reveals insanity. I've never said that in my life. I've never even thought it. I love being Jewish.

NANCY: Are you sure?

BEN: Yes, of course I'm sure! It's what I am! It's different! I can't be you, all blonde and blue eyed and vanilla.

(BEN *sees* NANCY's *reaction.*)

BEN: No! I didn't mean that! I meant, you're different from me, and I can't love me!

NANCY: So you'll settle for vanilla?

BEN: No, Nancy! I didn't mean it!

NANCY: I should go.

BEN: No! Don't go! Just give me a second to think!

NANCY: It's only getting worse.

BEN: No it's not. People say what they don't mean all the time, you know? It doesn't mean it's true. I could say I'm straight, and really be gay.

NANCY: What?

BEN: I could say I'm not gay, but be gay.

NANCY: Now what are you talking about?

BEN: I'm giving you an example.

NANCY: From where?

BEN: From when people say they're something that they're not. There are people out there who say that they're straight their whole lives and then they come out at the age of fifty, and everyone thinks "Oh yeah. We knew that guy was gay for fifty years."

NANCY: What are you telling me?

BEN: I'm not telling you anything.

NANCY: You're straight.

BEN: Yes, of course I'm straight.

NANCY: Do you sometimes think about being gay?

BEN: Yeah. I've thought about it. I've been attracted to men.

NANCY: Really?

BEN: Yes, everybody has. *(Pause)* Haven't they?

(She doesn't respond.)

BEN: People are sexual.

NANCY: Are you as attracted to men as you are to me?

BEN: No!

NANCY: How come you never tell me I'm pretty?

BEN: 'Cause you know you are.

NANCY: Do you think you're bi?

BEN: Well, I don't know. Maybe. I mean, who knows, right? That's my point. You don't know. And if you're really open to things, sometimes I think, "Yeah. Maybe I'm gay."

NANCY: Really?

BEN: Yeah. Maybe I am. The point is it doesn't matter what I say, like it doesn't matter that I said I don't want to be Jewish.

NANCY: And it doesn't matter what I said.

BEN: *(Hesitant)* Right. *(More confident)* Right.

NANCY: It doesn't matter, because we're saying it about ourselves and we could be wrong.

BEN: Right. You should never say anything about yourself, or anybody else, because people are always changing. You should only talk about things, like rocks, and Tonka Trucks. You shouldn't even ask people "How are you?" You should have to ask them "What did you just do?" *(Pause)* What?

NANCY: Nothing.

BEN: What are you thinking?

NANCY: I'm thinking about what you said.

BEN: What do you think?

NANCY: If I wanted you to know I'd be talking and I wouldn't be thinking, now wouldn't I?

BEN: Do you think I'm gay?

NANCY: No! Of course not!

BEN: You think I'm gay.

NANCY: No I don't.

BEN: Yes you do!

NANCY: How could you be gay? That's ridiculous! We couldn't make love the way we do if you were gay. It wouldn't be possible.

BEN: Well, I suppose it would be possible if I were bi.

NANCY: But you're not.

BEN: I don't think so.

NANCY: Would you stop saying "You don't think so!"

BEN: No. That's what I keep saying. It wouldn't be honest for me to say I'm anything.

NANCY: *(Beat)* I'm gonna go.

BEN: You can't go. It's three in the morning.

NANCY: I know, but I'm tired and I have a big day tomorrow. Three recipes are overdue, and the illustrator fell off her bike. I need to sleep.

BEN: So we'll sleep.

NANCY: No. I need to be in my own place.

BEN: Well how are you gonna get home?

NANCY: I'll take the train.

BEN: You can't take the train at three o'clock in the morning.

NANCY: Why not?

BEN: Because we're having a fight. You can't leave here and three weeks later turn up in the Hudson River. How do you think I'll feel?

NANCY: It's not all about you, Ben.

BEN: Take a cab.

NANCY: I'm not paying for a cab.

BEN: I'll pay for it.

NANCY: I don't want you paying for my cab. You're a graduate student.

BEN: Will you pay for it?

NANCY: Would you forget about the cab. I can get home by myself.

BEN: Fine. It's probably for the best. It's been six months. We had to clear the air.

NANCY: Yeah. Sometimes you gotta shake it up a little.

BEN: It's lucky we're not married. We'd have nowhere to go when we fight.

NANCY: Grace says there's no point in fighting if you're not married, because you can always find someone else.

BEN: Grace. There's a paradigm of relationship sensibility.

NANCY: Now you're insulting Grace? She's my best friend!

BEN: I know. Fine. Forget it.

NANCY: *(Leaving)* See you later.

BEN: Nancy!

NANCY: What?

BEN: Ninety-five percent of this evening was so fucking great!

NANCY: I know.

BEN: It's not every night we go out to dinner.

NANCY: And a movie.

BEN: And walking home through all the people.

NANCY: And eating ice-cream on your roof.

BEN: And seeing stars.

NANCY: And making love.

BEN: And you calling me a hook-nosed Jew.

(Pause)

NANCY: Goodnight. *(Exits)*

BEN: Goodnight.

(Blackout)

Scene Two

(Three A M. BEN's bed disappears. GENE and GRACE enter on Bed 2, stage right. GENE wears pajamas. GRACE wears lingerie. As the bed appears, GRACE is trying to force GENE to submit sexually.)

GENE: Come on, Grace… Stop… Stop! Grace, stop!

GRACE: Come on, Gene.

GENE: I'm not in the mood.

(GRACE *keeps trying.*)

GENE: Get offa me!

GRACE: Just a little.

GENE: No!

(GRACE *keeps trying*)

GENE: Would you get offa me! (*He throws her to the other side of the bed.*) Stay over there. Just stay over there!

GRACE: Why?

GENE: Because I need some air.

GRACE: Don't you like me?

GENE: Yeah, of course I like you, but gimme some air.

GRACE: Don't you wanna?

GENE: Yeah, I wanna, but couldn't we at least have a short conversation?

GRACE: We had a conversation!

GENE: You said "Hello."

GRACE: That's a short conversation.

GENE: I barely got into my pajamas.

GRACE: You don't need to wear them.

GENE: I like them. You're wearing that...shirt.

GRACE: It's lingerie. French. I got cold waiting for you, walking around...

GENE: Ohh, you weren't walkin' around naked, were you? Don't do that.

GRACE: Why not?

GENE: 'Cause you don't close the blinds. You don't even close the windows! People are gonna think you're a sex maniac.

GRACE: So? *(Flirting out the window)* Hello!

GENE: Don't say that. Some pervert's gonna climb in the window.

GRACE: What's wrong with that? *(Flirting out the window)*

GENE: *(Throwing her on the bed, away from the window)* Don't do that.

GRACE: *(Coyly making her way over to him)* Gene…

GENE: Stay there!

GRACE: Well, why'd you come over?

GENE: Because I wanted to see you.

GRACE: At three in the morning?

GENE: Some people work.

GRACE: I'm looking for a job!

GENE: I know, I know! I didn't mean that. How'd your interview go?

GRACE: I don't wanna talk about it.

GENE: Why not? What do you wanna talk about?

GRACE: Sex.

GENE: Ah Grace, we gotta talk about something else.

GRACE: Why? What's wrong with sex?

GENE: Nothing, but maybe we could have a few breaks in the rounds.

GRACE: How was your day?

GENE: No, see…look, I been coming here for five nights, and it's the same thing every night.

GRACE: Don't you like it?

GENE: Yeah, of course I like it. Why do you think I come here?

GRACE: I don't know.

GENE: 'Cause I like it. But maybe I like you a little too, and on the sixth night, we could pepper in some conversation.

GRACE: Gene, I told you this was not going to be serious.

GENE: I know, and that's fine.

GRACE: It's just temporary. You agreed.

GENE: Yes, I know. That's great. But even so, we could still have a little conversation.

GRACE: Tell me about your day.

GENE: No, see, that's what I'm saying. If it's just sex and my day, I'm not so interested.

GRACE: Don't you think I'm sexy?

GENE: Yes, of course I think you're sexy. You're incredibly sexy. Why am I here? Because you're so sexy-sexy. But you're also smart, you know, and it might add to the sex if you could use your smarts to tell me a little something about your life, 'cause then maybe I'd learn a little something about my life, see? That's how it works.

GRACE: No, Gene. It won't help you. My life is boring.

GENE: That's not what Mark tells me.

GRACE: Mark?

GENE: Yeah, he tells me you do very interesting things. He says you're very good at art.

GRACE: He said that?

GENE: Yes. He says you're very talented.

GRACE: That's sweet.

GENE: So tell me about art.

GRACE: Art is useless.

GENE: What do you mean art is useless? That's not true. Don't say that. Art is important.

GRACE: Oh really? Have you done a lot of art, Gene?

GENE: Come on. Don't talk to me like that. Just 'cause I didn't go to college doesn't mean I'm dumb.

GRACE: I didn't say you're dumb.

GENE: Tell me about art then.

GRACE: Well, where should we start? Would you prefer to know why the uniquely Italian spatial manipulation of iconographic imagery set a precedent for French classicists, or how Hans Holbein the Younger fused the High Renaissance with the Christian Humanism of Dürer?

GENE: Well…I don't know.

GRACE: That's my point, Gene. You think you want to have a conversation, but you don't.

GENE: Well, if you were really smart, you'd say it so I could understand it.

GRACE: Okay, Gene. You know what art is?

GENE: Yeah. Tell me.

GRACE: Imagine a little village where people wear a lot of shoes.

GENE: Okay.

GRACE: Can you see it?

GENE: Yeah.

GRACE: Imagine there's a couple of cobblers there who make all the shoes for everybody. They've been doing it their whole lives. They're the greatest cobblers in the world.

GENE: I could use a cobbler like that. I like nice shoes.

GRACE: Right. So one day in the village, nobody needs shoes anymore.

GENE: Why not?

GRACE: I don't know. They all went to the beach. But these two cobblers are the greatest cobblers, right?

GENE: They should retire.

GRACE: They don't want to retire. They want to make shoes.

GENE: But everyone's at the beach.

GRACE: Right, but they keep making them anyway, and gradually, since nobody needs to wear them, the shoes become very strange.

GENE: How do you mean?

GRACE: They don't fit anyone's feet. The cobblers make the heels too long and the straps too tight, and they don't care, 'cause no one's gonna wear them anyway. They just make them look the way they want 'em to look. And you know what?

GENE: What?

GRACE: People start buying them.

GENE: But they don't fit.

GRACE: Right. The people stick them on a table in their living-room, and they look at them.

GENE: But then they're not shoes anymore.

GRACE: Exactly. They're art.

(Pause)

GENE: Ohhhhhhh, I see. That's terrific. They were shoes, and then they're art. You see, now that's terrific. You're terrific. You're very smart.

GRACE: Yeah.

GENE: Yeah. And you know what?

GRACE: What?

GENE: It's sexy.

GRACE: Really?

GENE: Yeah. It's sexy to see you talkin' like that.

GRACE: *(Sexy)* Oh yeah?

GENE: *(Sexy)* Yeah.

GRACE: *(Making her way over to him)* Well then I'm glad I was talking like that.

GENE: Me too.

GRACE: 'Cause it kind of makes me want to have sex with you.

GENE: Yeah. Me too. *(Right before she kisses him)* Tell me something else.

GRACE: *(Throwing herself back)* Gene!!

GENE: What?

GRACE: I just told you a story.

GENE: So tell me another one.

GRACE: You only get one bedtime story, and then you have to fuck me.

GENE: You don't understand, Grace. I never went to college. I don't know people who talk like you.

GRACE: Don't you get what's attractive about you?

GENE: What?

GRACE: You're an adult.

GENE: That's not a very distinguishing feature.

GRACE: It is. Believe me. All those college boys you think are so great, they don't even get out of school 'til they're thirty. Adolescence is an eternal state in this

country. I'm thirty years old, dating sniveling little
boys.

GENE: Yeah, but...

GRACE: But nothing. You are the first *man* I have dated.
And we're not even dating. We're just having this
thing, but you are the first *man* I've even had a thing
with. And *Men*, big, strong *men* like you, who know
what they want, and don't spend all night whining,
(Whines) "I don't know what I want to do with my
life—" Do you know that I have actually been with
guys who want *me* to tell them what they should do
with their lives? Can you believe that? You never asked
me that.

GENE: I've only known you for five days.

GRACE: But you wouldn't ask me that, because you're
tough, you're a man from the street, and it's sexy.

GENE: Really?

GRACE: Yeah. I was thinking about you just today.

GENE: You were?

GRACE: Yeah. In my interview.

GENE: Oh yeah. How'd it go?

GRACE: No Gene, see, you think you want to hear
about my life, but you don't.

GENE: Grace, I guarantee you, whatever happened in
that interview will turn me on.

GRACE: I don't think so.

GENE: If you tell me, I'll wanna have sex with you.

GRACE: Really?

GENE: I'll wanna rip you to pieces. Now what
happened?

GRACE: You promise to rip me to pieces?

(GENE *nods affirmatively.*)

GRACE: It's really very small.

GENE: Then I'll rip you into little pieces.

GRACE: Okay. I had this problem when the boss was talking that happens to me sometimes when I get nervous.

GENE: What?

GRACE: I get this tickle under my uvula.

GENE: Your what?

GRACE: My uvula. *(Sensing his curiosity)* That's a big word.

GENE: What is it?

GRACE: A *uvula*?

GENE: Yeah.

GRACE: It sounds like a female sex word. Doesn't it? *Uvula.*

GENE: What is it?

GRACE: *(Sensually)* It's onomatopoetic. *Uvula.*

GENE: What is that?!

GRACE: Why a *uvula* is that thick flap of skin that hangs down in the back of your throat. It even looks like a female sex part. Don't you think? *(She opens her mouth to show him)* Can you see it? *(Shows him again)*

GENE: *(Checking)* No. The light's not good.

GRACE: You can't see my *uvula*?

GENE: Where was the tickle?

GRACE: Under my *uvula*.

GENE: So what happened? You couldn't concentrate?

GRACE: I guess. I'm having problems concentrating right now.

GENE: But what happened?

GRACE: I don't know, Gene. Who cares?

GENE: I care.

GRACE: Then rip me to pieces.

GENE: Tell me the story.

GRACE: *Uvula*.

GENE: Grace...

GRACE: *Onomatopoetic*?

GENE: What happened in the interview?

GRACE: Oh Jesus Christ Gene! Give it a break! It's the middle of the night. We're alone in a bed. Enough with the mind. On to the body. I'm getting blue ovaries!

GENE: But I'm curious about your aspirations.

GRACE: And I'm curious about your cock!

GENE: Grace! Don't you want to be with someone better than you?

GRACE: No. I want to be with you! Now rip me to pieces!

GENE: But I always wanted to be with someone more educated than me, so I could elevate myself. Don't you feel that?

GRACE: Well I guess eventually it would be nice to be with someone smart.

(GENE *looks demolished.*)

GRACE: Oh no, Gene, I didn't mean it that way. You're smart. Really. Very smart. Don't obsess about the college thing. It's stupid. Really. See, this is why we shouldn't talk. You're great, Gene. All the things Mark has told me are true, the way you got a job, took care of him, put him through college. That's smart.

GENE: I didn't have a choice.

GRACE: And that's the adult reaction. You did what you had to do.

GENE: I wish I went to college and Mark was the hitman.

GRACE: Maybe he'd be Clean Mark the Killing Machine.

GENE: I don't thinks so.

GRACE: But you're Clean Gene!

GENE: Yeah.

GRACE: And everyone's afraid of Clean Gene.

GENE: Sort of.

GRACE: What do you mean "sort of?"

GENE: They don't take the Dutch seriously.

GRACE: They're Mafia!

GENE: But they're not Italian. My boss's name is Rut *(Pronounced "Root")*. Who ever heard of a Mafia Don named Rut?

GRACE: There's Dutch Schultz.

GENE: He was big time. My guys are small. There's only three of them. Rut, Hecka Herrit, and Jap *(Pronounced "Yawp")*.

GRACE: You're Italian.

GENE: I know, but I didn't make it at first with the Garbolenies, so the Italian guys don't think I deserve it.

GRACE: Who says that?

GENE: I hear it around.

GRACE: You tell me which ones.

GENE: No. It's stupid. I'm just saying I'm not as tough as you make me out.

GRACE: Are you kidding? When I saw you at Mimi's party I said, "Who is that tough guy?" I couldn't figure out what you were doing at that party.

GENE: I whacked Mimi's brother.

GRACE: You see? Every second I interview for a dumb advertising-sticker job, you are out on the street making life and death decisions. Do you not appreciate the gravity of what you do?

GENE: Yeah, but I don't decide who gets whacked. I just whack 'em. And it's routine, you know? I've got my thing.

GRACE: The plastic bag.

GENE: Yeah, the plastic bag. I tie 'em up, plastic bag 'em, leave the room, and five minutes later they're blue. No muss, no fuss.

GRACE: Clean Gene the Killing Machine.

GENE: Yeah, but it gets old.

GRACE: No, Gene. Don't say that. Why would you say that?

GENE: It's been building up.

GRACE: Don't be a sniveling boy.

GENE: I'm not. I'm trying to tell you something.

GRACE: I don't want to hear it, Gene. Play your strong hand.

GENE: But you get me thinking, Grace.

GRACE: Well don't. What did you do today?

GENE: I don't want to talk about it.

GRACE: Why not?

GENE: I don't like it.

GRACE: I do.

GENE: Don't say that.

GRACE: You don't want to talk about my two favorite subjects, murder and sex.

GENE: Shh! Don't say that!

GRACE: Even the words?

GENE: I like to talk about things I can't do or don't do, 'cause I don't get the chance to do 'em.

GRACE: Okay, fine. So let's just do it, if that's what you like.

GENE: Yeah. That's what I like.

GRACE: *(Sexy)* What do you like?

GENE: I like to just…

GRACE: Yeah?

GENE: Lemme turn out the light.

GRACE: No! Don't turn out the light! Talk to me.

GENE: I thought you liked me 'cause I don't talk.

GRACE: About certain things, Gene, like "what are you going to do with the rest of your life." That doesn't interest me, okay? I wanna fuck and fight, and talk about whacking and sex.

GENE: Yeah, but I'm…

GRACE: What?

GENE: …thinking of making a change.

GRACE: What kind of a change?

GENE: A job change.

GRACE: Geeeene!!!

GENE: What?

GRACE: You are the only hitman I've ever slept with! Do you have any clue how fucking sexy that is?!!

GENE: Is that why you're with me? 'Cause I'm a hitman?

GRACE: No, baby, I'm with you 'cause you're...well... yeah.

GENE: That's sick.

GRACE: No. You're different. Didn't you hear me?

GENE: Yeah, but can't I be different without whacking people?

GRACE: What else are you gonna do?

GENE: I don't know. I thought maybe you'd have some ideas.

GRACE: AAAAAAAHHHHHHHHH!!!

GENE: What?!

GRACE: You're doing it!

GENE: What?!

GRACE: You're asking me to tell you what to do with your life, like the sniveling boys.

GENE: No, I'm not. I'm not!

GRACE: Why can't you tell me about whacking, and fuck me?

GENE: 'Cause sometimes I think there's more to life.

GRACE: AAAAAAAHHHHHHH!!!

GENE: What?

GRACE: Get out.

GENE: No, wait.

GRACE: I've been very clear with you, Gene. If I want talking, I can date my brother.

GENE: No. Wait a second.

GRACE: This was about change, Gene. This was about sexy, tough guy. This wasn't about "what am I going to do with the rest of my life".

GENE: Maybe we'll talk in the morning.

GRACE: No! We're not talking! You have to go to work, and I have to think, so just get out.

GENE: Wait a second.

GRACE: No. I've waited too long. Get out. I have a throbbing headache.

GENE: Really?

GRACE: No. But get out.

GENE: Okay, okay, forget it. I'll say what you want me to say. Just let me spend the night, okay? We'll do whatever you want.

GRACE: Sex too?

GENE: Having or talking?

GRACE: Okay, we can just do it. I'm capable of compromise. You don't have to talk about it, but we have to do it. A lot. And you have to talk about whacking.

GENE: *(Despondent)* Alright.

GRACE: Now what happened today? You chased a guy.

GENE: I chased a guy.

GRACE: Up until tonight?

GENE: Yeah. All day and tonight.

GRACE: A car chase?

GENE: An everything chase. Car, train, and foot.

GRACE: Wow.

GENE: Yeah. He was dusting his tracks. He started out in Brooklyn, he ran to Queens, and he ended up in the Bronx.

GRACE: Is that where you caught him?

GENE: Yeah.

GRACE: Did you take him back to your office?

GENE: No. They had a place in the Bronx.

GRACE: So where'd you put him?

GENE: They had a machine.

GRACE: What kind of machine?

GENE: You know.

GRACE: An incinerator?

GENE: Yeah.

GRACE: Did you put him in whole?

GENE: It doesn't work like that.

GRACE: Did you cut him up?

GENE: I'm Clean Gene.

GRACE: You could put down newspaper.

GENE: It's not an art project.

GRACE: I know.

GENE: And gettin' rid of him wasn't the scary part.

GRACE: What was?

GENE: His partner got away.

GRACE: You didn't get him?

GENE: No, and they're brothers, which makes it real bad.

GRACE: Why?

GENE: 'Cause vengeance is mine saith the brother.

GRACE: He's on the loose?

GENE: Yeah.

GRACE: Is he gonna come after you?

GENE: It wouldn't be smart if he did, but he might.

GRACE: Does he know where you live?

GENE: No.

GRACE: He doesn't know where I live, does he?

GENE: No.

(The front door buzzer buzzes. GRACE *nearly leaps out of her skin.)*

GRACE: Aaahh!! What's that?!!

GENE: *(Alert)* The door.

GRACE: At three in the morning?

GENE: *(Pulling his gun from his pile of clothes)* Stay here.

GRACE: No, I'll come!

GENE: Stay here!

GRACE: It's my apartment!

GENE: I'll get it!

GRACE: I'll stay behind you.

GENE: It's not a game.

GRACE: What if it's a friend of mine?

GENE: Then I'll let 'em in.

GRACE: No! They'll take one look at you, and they'll think you killed me.

GENE: Why? What do I look like?

GRACE: A hitman.

GENE: *(Despondent)* Shit.

(The buzzer buzzes again.)

GRACE: Aaahh!!

GENE: *(Alert)* Get in the closet.

GRACE: In the closet?

GENE: Yes. In the closet.

GRACE: I'll just go into the bathroom, so I can hear.

(Banging on the door is heard.)

GRACE: Aaaaahhh!!

GENE: Shh!

GRACE: It's like The Godfather.

GENE: It's like reality.

(More banging)

GRACE: Aaaaaahhh!!

GENE: If you don't get in the closet I'm gonna tie you up!

GRACE: Okay. Okay. *(She extends her wrists to be tied up. He carries her to the closet.)* You don't have to tie me up.

GENE: I'll be back.

GRACE: Okay.

(GRACE steps in the closet. GENE closes the door. More banging.)

GRACE: Aaaaahhh!!

(GRACE bursts out of the closet and collapses in GENE's arms.)

GENE: *(Hissing)* Keep quiet! Everything will be alright, but listen, even if it seems like a long time, stay in the closet. Okay? I'll case the room. *(No response)* Okay?

GRACE: Okay.

GENE: I'll be right back.

(GENE closes the closet door, and exits stageright. GRACE sticks her head out of the closet. She's grown impatient. She squiggles out, and listens.)

NANCY: *(Offstage)* Aaaahhh!

GENE: *(Offstage)* Quiet! Who sent you?!

NANCY: *(Offstage)* Aaaahhh!

GENE: *(Offstage)* Keep quiet!

NANCY: *(Offstage)* Who are you? What have you done? Where's Grace?

GRACE: Nancy! *(She runs off stage right.)*

GENE: *(Offstage)* I'm Gene. I haven't done anything.

GRACE: *(Offstage)* Nancy!

NANCY: *(Offstage)* Grace! What's going on? Why does he have a gun?

GRACE: *(Offstage)* It's okay. He's a friend of mine.

NANCY: *(Offstage)* That's a big gun.

GRACE: *(Offstage)* He's a big guy.

GENE: *(Offstage)* Why aren't you in the closet?

GRACE: *(Offstage)* I heard it was Nancy. Here. Come in.

(They enter. NANCY is wary of GENE.)

GRACE: Nancy, this is Gene. Gene, Nancy.

GENE: *(Extending his hand)* Hi. Nice to meet you.

NANCY: *(Taking his hand)* Hi.

GRACE: Nancy went to college.

GENE: Oh. Are you acquainted with the shoe theory?

NANCY: The what?

GRACE: She's not in art, Gene. She just went to college.

GENE: What do you do?

NANCY: I edit cookbooks.

GENE: Oh. Very nice. *(He turns his back to put his gun in his pile of clothes.)*

GRACE: *(Mouthing with delight)* He's a hitman!

NANCY: *(Mouthing)* What?!

GRACE: *(Whispering)* He's a HITMAN! And he's my therapist's brother. He's been trying to set us up for ages. I just want a short-term thing, but he might want more. I'll tell you later.

(NANCY can't take her eyes off GENE, who's dealing with the complex cartridges and mutes and clicks of his gun.)

GRACE: So what are you doing here?

NANCY: Uh. I don't know. I'm a little frazzled.

GENE: *(Turning around to NANCY)* Excuse me. I don't mean to interrupt, but… *(Turning to GRACE and whispering loudly)* …it's bothering me that I told you to stay in the closet and you didn't.

GRACE: *(In a loud whisper)* I heard it was Nancy.

GENE: *(In a loud whisper)* No you didn't.

GRACE: Yes I did.

GENE: When the gun comes out, I'm in charge.

GRACE: Okay, fine.

(They both turn to face NANCY.)

GRACE: Now what were you saying?

NANCY: Uhh…

GENE: Let us retire into the living room.

GRACE: No. It's cold.

GENE: Well we cannot stay here. We are in our pajamas

GRACE: So what? It's just Nancy. *(To NANCY)* He's a little old-fashioned. He doesn't even swear.

GENE: There is nowhere to sit. There is only the bed.

GRACE: So we'll sit on the bed.

GENE: I am not going to do that.

GRACE: *(Turning on the light and sitting with* NANCY *on the bed)* Fine. *(Throwing a pillow on the floor)* Sitteth on the floor. *(To* NANCY*)* Now what happened?

*(*GENE *turns to his pile of clothes and puts away his gun.)*

NANCY: *(Looking at* GENE*)* Can we talk in front of Gene?

GRACE: He's okay. Believe me. He runs with a different crowd. And most of them aren't running anymore.

GENE: *(Turning)* Would you like me to step out?

GRACE: No. You're fine. *(To* NANCY*)* He's fine, isn't he? I had a little scare when you rang, and he makes me feel safe. Plus, he likes hearing educated people talk.

GENE: I am happy to leave.

NANCY: No. Stay.

GENE: I will be very quiet. *(He sits on the floor.)*

NANCY: *(After they're settled.)* Ben is gay.

GRACE: What?!

NANCY: Ben. He's gay. He's Ben. He's Bengay.

GRACE: What are you talking about? Who did he sleep with?

NANCY: No one yet, but he said tonight "I think I might be gay."

GRACE: He did?

NANCY: Yes. From out of nowhere. We were having this fight...

GRACE: About what?

NANCY: About nothing, you know, a late night fight about who are you and who am I. And out of nowhere he says "It doesn't matter what we say we are because people are always wrong about themselves. I could say I'm straight but really be gay."

GRACE: He said that?

NANCY: Yes.

GRACE: He meant it as an example.

NANCY: Out of nowhere like that? And then I say "Are you gay?" or "Have you ever thought about it?", and he says "Yes, I've been attracted to men, I always assumed I'd have an encounter with a man, and sometimes I think `Yeah, maybe I'm gay.'"

GRACE: That doesn't make him gay.

NANCY: It's a pretty strong case.

GRACE: What do you think, Gene?

GENE: I don't know.

GRACE: Have you ever thought about men?

GENE: No.

NANCY: And he never tells me I'm sexy or beautiful or anything. I mean, shouldn't he say that? Is there something wrong with me? Aren't I attractive?

GRACE: Yes Nancy, you're beautiful! Isn't she beautiful, Gene?

GENE: Yeah. You're beautiful. You're really beautiful. You got a great—

GRACE: Alright, Gene!

NANCY: Well don't you think it's weird he would bring it up like that, and then hedge around? You do hear about people who fight it their whole lives. It starts with wondering, and then maybe talking about it, and then they have one experience, and then a few more, and then they're trying to repress it, and finally they're fifty years old, and they can't keep it in any more. They're just gay. And their poor wives who have trusted them their whole lives, and tried to believe in them, are destroyed. I don't want to be like that.

GRACE: You don't know he's gay just from that. We've fooled around with women and we're not gay.

NANCY: It's different with women.

GENE: You did?

GRACE: In college. Everyone did.

GENE: Really?

GRACE: All the women. Yeah.

GENE: You and Nancy?

GRACE: Not together, but separately.

NANCY: What am I going to do?

GENE: College.

NANCY: I went home, and I couldn't fall asleep.

GRACE: Of course.

NANCY: I've been pacing around the kitchen like an animal. I didn't know what to do, so I came over.

GRACE: You were right to come over. You'll spend the night.

GENE: With us?

GRACE: You can sleep on the couch.

GENE: While you sleep with Nancy?

GRACE & NANCY: We're not going to fool around, Gene!

GRACE: She's in distress. Can't you see that? *(Sudden idea)* I know what we should do!

NANCY: What?

GRACE: We'll call Mark.

GENE: Oh no.

GRACE: He's gay. Maybe he would know.

GENE: We're not calling him.

NANCY: Who is he?

GRACE: Gene's brother.

NANCY: Your therapist?

GRACE: Yeah. He's sort of my friend too.

GENE: Forget about it. We're not calling him. It's three o'clock in the morning.

GRACE: He doesn't care. He's up late.

NANCY: Does a good therapist set his patient up with his brother?

GRACE: He's not a good therapist.

GENE: What are you talking about?! He's an excellent therapist!

GRACE: He's a little young. I just pay him to be my friend for an hour a week. He helps me with my narcicism. Sometimes I don't even pay him. We just go for coffee.

GENE: He's the best therapist in the business.

GRACE: And he's gay.

GENE: We're not calling him.

NANCY: Your brother is gay?

GENE: Yeah, you got a problem with that?!

NANCY: No, no. Not at all.

GRACE: We'll tell him the situation and ask him what he thinks.

GENE: He is not a typical gay person.

GRACE: He's as gay as anyone else.

GENE: We're not calling him. It's three in the morning. Forget it.

GRACE: Listen to you. Ordering us around.

GENE: He's *my* brother.

GRACE: I knew him before I knew you, and I know him better than I know you.

GENE: Well I knew him before I knew any of you, so I know him the best.

GRACE: *(To* NANCY*)* Men are so competitive.

NANCY: What's not typical about him?

GRACE: He has a weird fetish.

GENE: It's not a fetish.

GRACE: He likes certain kinds of men.

NANCY: What kinds?

GENE: What difference does it make? Everybody likes certain kinds of people.

GRACE: His taste runs specific.

NANCY: What is it?

GENE: It's none of your business.

GRACE: Mark doesn't hide it. Why should you?

GENE: It is not your responsibility to advertise my brother's interests.

NANCY: Come on, Gene. I don't care. I don't even know him.

GRACE: He likes older men.

GENE: Grace!

NANCY: So what? So do I.

GRACE: A lot older.

GENE: So what?

NANCY: How old?

GENE: What difference does it make?

GRACE: *Very* old.

NANCY: Really?

GRACE: Yes. Gene's a little protective.

GENE: I don't think it makes any difference...

NANCY: Seventies?

GRACE: And up.

NANCY: *Eighties?!*

GRACE: As high as he can get 'em.

NANCY: *Nineties?!*

GRACE: If they're still kickin'.

NANCY: That's amazing.

GENE: My brother, the freak show.

GRACE: He is not.

GENE: The way you talk about him.

GRACE: I appreciate him.

NANCY: So do I.

GENE: Like the bearded lady.

GRACE: No. For who he is. I don't think there's anything wrong with it. It's just unusual. It's funny. You have no sense of humor.

NANCY: Let's call him.

GENE: I told you. He does not represent the gay community.

NANCY: Apparently not.

GRACE: But he's a very nice person, with very good instincts. He's a professional, he stays up late, and I know he'd love to talk to us.

GENE: You'll wake him up.

GRACE: You know he's awake.

GENE: At three in the morning?!

GRACE: Would you stop saying what time it is!

NANCY: It is true, Gene, that a gay person might have a better sense of this than we do. And he is a therapist.

GRACE: She needs to know.

NANCY: I could use a good opinion.

GRACE: He has very good judgement, in spite of what I said.

NANCY: Please Gene. It's important.

GRACE: Look at her. She's desperate. She's pathetic. Can you imagine a similar anxiety about the love of your life?

GENE: I already know you slept with women.

GRACE: I didn't know I was the love of your life.

GENE: You're not.

GRACE: Then why did you say that?

GENE: What difference does it make?

GRACE: Gene, you have only known me for five nights.

GENE: I have fast feelings.

GRACE: Gene…

GENE: Don't start thinking you're the love of my life. I didn't say that. But don't tell me you're not either.

GRACE: Do you love me, Gene?

GENE: Of course not! I barely know you! I don't love anybody. I'm Clean Gene!

NANCY: Could we make the call?

GRACE: Gene, I'm shocked. I thought I was very clear.

GENE: Yeah, you were. Forget it, okay? Just forget it. I don't even know what I'm talking about.

NANCY: Can we please call your brother?

GENE: Yeah, call him. Fine. Do whatever you want.

GRACE: We can put him on speaker-phone.

NANCY: Thank you, Gene.

GRACE: *(Dialing)* This'll be great. He'll be great.

Scene Three

(Bed 3 enters stageleft with MARK *and* MR ABRAMSON *under the sheets. We hear the phone ring.)*

*(*MARK *and* MR ABRAMSON *appear.)*

MR ABRAMSON: Don't answer that.

*(*MARK *and* MR ABRAMSON *disappear under the sheets. The phone rings.)*

MR ABRAMSON: Wrong number.

(It rings again.)

MARK: *(Reappearing)* I have to get it. It could be a patient. It could be an emergency.

MR ABRAMSON: But we were going so good.

MARK: We'll start again.

MR ABRAMSON: I'll have to rerev my engine. I'll have to kickstart it.

MARK: *(Into telephone)* Hello?

GRACE: Mark, it's Grace.

MARK: Grace. You're calling late. Is everything all right?

GRACE: Well, I'm here with a friend.

MARK: Gene?

GENE: *(To* MARK*)* I told her not to call.

MARK: Oh I'm so happy. How's it going for you two? Everything working out?

GENE: It would be a lot better if Grace would—

GRACE: It's not about us, Mark. I have another friend here with a problem.

GENE: *(To* MARK*)* Are we waking you? We can call back another time. I know you need your sleep.

MARK: Come on, Gene. I'm not twelve.

MR ABRAMSON: What's happening?

MARK: Just a minute.

MR ABRAMSON: A minute for me is a valuable commodity.

GRACE: We have a question to ask you.

MARK: What?

GENE: I said just 'cause you're gay doesn't mean we should ask. I told her Mark, just like you said.

MARK: What are you talking about?

GRACE: My friend, Nancy, has a question.

MARK: Are you on speaker-phone?

GRACE: Yes.

MR ABRAMSON: What's going on?

MARK: Hang on Grace. *(To* MR ABRAMSON*)* I don't know. My brother and a friend are on speaker-phone.

MR ABRAMSON: I was so close.

MARK: Just a second.

MR ABRAMSON: I haven't been this close since 1962.

MARK: Will you wait one second. *(Into phone)* What's your question?

GRACE: Nancy has the question, and Gene and I are her support.

MARK: Shoot.

GRACE: *(To* NANCY*)* Say "hi".

NANCY: Hi.

MARK: Hi Nancy. How are you?

NANCY: Fine.

MARK: What's the matter?

MR ABRAMSON: What's the matter?

MARK: *(To* MR ABRAMSON*)* It's the friend of a patient of mine who's sleeping with my brother. Just a second.

GRACE: Are you alone?

MARK: No. I have a friend here.

GENE: Oh great.

GRACE: Is your friend gay?

MARK: *(Looking at* MR ABRAMSON *beside him in bed)* Yes he is.

MR ABRAMSON: What?

MARK: You're gay.

GENE: You know, we can call back another time.

GRACE: Your friend can participate.

MARK: Okay. *(To* MR ABRAMSON*)* You can participate.

MR ABRAMSON: In what?

MARK: I don't know.

GRACE: We want to know if someone is gay.

MARK: Are you gay, Nancy?

NANCY: No.

MR ABRAMSON: What's going on?

MARK: *(To* MR ABRAMSON*)* They want to know if someone is gay.

MR ABRAMSON: Who?

MARK: I don't know.

GRACE: Is that your friend?

MARK: Yes.

GRACE: Put him on.

GENE: We don't need to talk to him.

MR ABRAMSON: *(Putting the phone to his ear)* Hello?

GRACE: Hello? Who's this?

MR ABRAMSON: Donald Abramson.

GRACE: Hi Donald. My name is Grace, and this is Nancy. Say "hi", Nancy.

NANCY: Hi.

MR ABRAMSON: Hello, Grace. Hello, Nancy.

GRACE: And Gene.

GENE: Hello.

MR ABRAMSON: Hello, Gene.

GRACE: Gene is Mark's brother.

MR ABRAMSON: Yes. I've heard of him. You're the hitman, right?

GENE: What do you mean I'm the hitman? I'm other things too.

MR ABRAMSON: But you are a hitman.

GRACE: Yes, of course he is.

MR ABRAMSON: What's it like to whack?

GENE: Put my brother on the phone.

MR ABRAMSON: Do you shoot them?

GENE: Get my brother or I'll shoot you!

MR ABRAMSON: Okay, okay! Don't get excited! *(Handing phone to* MARK*)* The hitman wants to talk to you.

GRACE: He's an old man. You'll give him a heart attack.

MARK: *(Into phone)* What?

GENE: Why do you tell everyone I'm a hitman?

MARK: You are.

GENE: I don't tell everyone you're gay.

MARK: Well that's not my profession, Gene. I'm a therapist. I don't tell everyone you're straight. And anyway, we can't hide from our labels.

GENE: Don't start that with me.

MARK: You're so proud of me, Gene, but when I practice on you, you get defensive. I know you want to change. I want you to change too. That's why I set you up with Grace.

GENE: Grace wants me to be a serial killer.

GRACE: I do not.

NANCY: Can I ask my question?

GRACE: Right. Nancy. We're forgetting about Nancy.

MR ABRAMSON: *(To* MARK*)* Can I listen? I won't insult him.

MARK: *(Handing him the phone)* Here.

MR ABRAMSON: *(Sweetly into phone)* Hello?

GRACE: Nancy has a question for both of you.

MR ABRAMSON: All right. *(To* MARK*)* Nancy has a question for you and me.

GRACE: Don't you have speaker-phone over there?

MR ABRAMSON: *(To* MARK, *who tickles him)* Do we have a speaker-phone?

MARK: No. (MR ABRAMSON *giggles.*)

GRACE: What's going on over there?

MR ABRAMSON: *(Into phone, giggling)* No. We do not have a speaker-phone.

GRACE: Could you put Mark back on the phone?

MR ABRAMSON: What's the matter with me?

GRACE: We just want to talk to Mark for a second.

MR ABRAMSON: *(Handing* MARK *the phone)* Alright, here. She wants to talk to you. I don't see what's the matter with me.

MARK: What's up, Grace?

GRACE: Nancy has her question.

MARK: What is it, Nancy?

NANCY: I think my boyfriend is gay.

MARK: Oh? Why do you think that?

NANCY: He said tonight he thinks he's gay.

MARK: That's a good sign.

GRACE: But that's not the whole story.

MARK: What else?

MR ABRAMSON: What are they saying?

MARK: *(To* MR ABRAMSON*)* Nancy's boyfriend told her he thinks he's gay.

MR ABRAMSON: ooHoo.

GRACE: But it was in context.

MARK: What was the context?

GRACE: They were having a fight.

GENE: Would you let Nancy tell it. It's her story.

GRACE: I want him to know the context.

GENE: Nancy can tell him the context. Go ahead, Nancy. Tell him the context.

NANCY: We were having a late-night fight about who we really are, and he said you could never say who you really are, because some people say they're not gay their whole lives and then they come out.

MARK: That's true.

MR ABRAMSON: What's true?

MARK: The boyfriend said you can say you're straight but really be gay.

MR ABRAMSON: That's true.

NANCY: Right. Why would he say that all of a sudden?

MARK: It is a good example of his point.

NANCY: But when I asked him why he said it and whether he thought he was gay, he said maybe he was, he really couldn't say.

MARK: That sounds more like a point he was trying to make.

NANCY: But when I asked him if he'd ever thought about men, he said he had, and he always assumed he'd have a gay encounter.

MARK: Straight guy experimenting.

NANCY: What?

MR ABRAMSON: What?

MARK: The boyfrend said he assumed at some point he'd have a gay encounter.

MR ABRAMSON: Aah yes. One of those.

MARK: Classic.

NANCY: Classic what?

MARK: Classic straight guy experimenting.

GRACE: Classic!

NANCY: You think so?

MARK: Absolutely.

MR ABRAMSON: Classic.

MARK: Mister Abramson agrees.

NANCY: But don't you think that sometimes repressed homosexuals let it out a little at a time? Like they experiment once, let it go, try it again, like it more than women…

MARK: What kind of sex do you have?

NANCY: What do you mean?

MARK: Is it good?

GENE: I don't think we need to know that.

MARK: Is that my brother?

GRACE: Yes. He's embarrassed.

MARK: Good. This is good for you, Genie.

GENE: We don't need to know about her bed-life.

GRACE: He can't even say sex.

MARK: If we want to get to the root of the problem we do. So what's your sex like?

GENE: Come on, Mark. Give it a break.

MARK: Gene, Gene, Gene. Always the older brother. You have to protect everybody.

GRACE: Except for the guys he whacks.

MARK: Maybe that's why he's so protective of everyone else.

GENE: I am not the subject of this conversation.

NANCY: Maybe this isn't working out.

MARK: How's your sex life?

GENE: We don't need to know!

MARK: You didn't need to know about me until you saw for yourself.

GRACE: What did you see?

GENE: Nothing.

MARK: Grade school kissing games where the girls chase after the boys and kiss them.

GRACE: What's wrong with that?

GENE: He was the head of the girls!

GRACE: *(Seeing* NANCY'*s distress)* We have to talk about Nancy.

MARK: All I'm saying is we're like doctors. And if we want to solve the problem, we may have to look at the body. Tell us about your sex.

NANCY: Our sex is great! Okay? It's the best. It's very exciting.

MARK: Then don't worry about it.

MR ABRAMSON: Worry about what?

MARK: Her great sex.

NANCY: But that's the problem. It makes me feel weird.

MARK: Why?

NANCY: Because if he really is gay, I feel betrayed.

MR ABRAMSON: What's she saying?

MARK: She says they have great sex, and that's why she feels so weird.

MR ABRAMSON: Betrayed.

MARK: That's exactly what she said. Did you hear that?

MR ABRAMSON: No.

MARK: That was very good.

MR ABRAMSON: You should see me when I can hear.

NANCY: I feel like who is this person? Or what did all that mean? Was he pretending all that time in order to prove something? And then tonight, he totally lost interest right at the end.

MARK: Really?

NANCY: Yeah. He stopped and got all freaked out.

MARK: He's gay. *(To* MR ABRAMSON*)* Tonight he stopped right at the end and freaked out.

MR ABRAMSON: Homo.

MARK: *(On phone)* Mister Abramson says he's a homo.

NANCY: I guess he is. And that means that all these months of hot sex…

GRACE: Just a show.

GENE: You don't know that.

MARK: In the sex, you're sure he was with it?

NANCY: Yeah, yeah, he was great. We'd grunt and grind, and I'd talk dirty.

GRACE: You did?

NANCY: Yeah.

GRACE: What did you say?

NANCY: The usual.

GRACE: *(To* GENE*)* That's all I'm asking for.

MARK: And he liked it?

NANCY: I think so. He didn't say much.

MARK: Hmm…

MR ABRAMSON: What?

MARK: They had hot sex and she'd talk dirty, but he wouldn't say much.

MR ABRAMSON: Hmm…

NANCY: Sometimes he'd say "rape me".

MARK: Really?

NANCY: Yeah.

MR ABRAMSON: What?

GRACE: Really?

GENE: The guy said that?

NANCY: Yeah.

MARK: He could be more than gay.

MR ABRAMSON: Put me on.

(MARK *hands phone to* MR ABRAMSON.)

MR ABRAMSON: Nancy? Is that your name? Nancy?

NANCY: Yes.

MR ABRAMSON: Listen to me, Nancy. I've been around the block a few times.

GRACE: I'll bet.

MR ABRAMSON: If you talk dirty and he doesn't, if he stops right at the end, even if he hasn't in the past, and if he says "some people are straight but really they're gay", he's crying out to you. He's gay.

NANCY: But I love him!

MR ABRAMSON: You can't love him as a lover if he's not the lover you think you thought you loved.

NANCY: *(After a beat)* What?

GRACE: We should call him.

MR ABRAMSON: That's a good idea.

GENE: That's a bad idea.

NANCY: No.

GRACE: *(To* NANCY*)* Why not?

MARK: What's a good idea?

MR ABRAMSON: *(To* MARK*)* We're gonna call him.

NANCY: I don't want to talk to him.

MARK: That's a bad idea. Give me the phone.

GRACE: Why not? We'll be right here for you. We'll have him on speaker-phone.

GENE: You can't gang up on him like that. It's his own affair.

GRACE: We're friends. Give me the phone

MR ABRAMSON: Sure. We're friends.

MARK: You can't do that to the guy.

GENE: You can't do that to the guy.

MR ABRAMSON: Sure you can.

NANCY: He'll get nasty.

MARK: You'll corner him.

GRACE: Not with us here. It's better. You won't get all tangled up like you do when you're alone.

MR ABRAMSON: Talking is very important.

MARK: He shouldn't have to talk to the whole world.

NANCY: He'll feel trapped.

GENE: It's not right.

MARK: What's happening? Give me the phone.

GRACE: He can always hang up.

GENE: None of this is our business.

GRACE: Nancy, you know it's more objective with other people.

NANCY: Stop! I can't do it! I can't talk to him. He'll freak out!

MARK: Nancy?

NANCY: Yes?

MARK: It's Mark.

NANCY: Hi Mark.

MARK: We don't have to call him. It's late, and we're all tired. You'll have to find some time after a day or two to talk to him quietly and alone. And do it during the day, not at night.

GENE: You see? That's a professional talking.

GRACE: Mark! I can't believe what a fuddy-duddy you are! Let's call him now. We have three-way calling. It'll be like group therapy. What's his number?

GENE: Don't tell her, Nancy.

NANCY: I don't want to do it.

GRACE: Why not? There is a reason why people talk in groups. We'll get it all cleared up.

NANCY: I don't want to do it.

GRACE: You know how you are. You'll just keep stewing until it comes out.

GENE: That's her business.

MR ABRAMSON: What's happening?

MARK: They're fighting over whether or not we should call the boyfriend.

MR ABRAMSON: Of course we should.

MARK: I don't think so.

MR ABRAMSON: What do you know?

GRACE: People don't always know what's best for them, and that's what friends are for. (*To* NANCY)

Don't you remember our counselling class? "Alone at night, fight. Talk together, fairer weather."

GENE: You never told me you took a counselling class.

GRACE: I never told you anything.

GENE: How come you don't counsel me?

GRACE: Because you're my lover, Gene, not my friend.

GENE: But if you took it in a class…

GRACE: I use it for my past, Gene, not my present, okay? Nancy is my past.

MR ABRAMSON: What's happening?

MARK: They're still arguing.

GENE: I can't talk about my professional concerns, but you can ask her boyfriend about his bed-life?

GRACE: Sex-life, Gene! Would you just say sex! It's liberating!

GENE: There's too many people here.

MR ABRAMSON: Gimme the phone. *(Taking the phone from* MARK*)* Hello? Is anybody there?

GENE, GRACE & NANCY: Yeah!

MR ABRAMSON: Are you still fighting? Can you hear me?

GENE: Of course we hear you. You're talking into a telephone.

MR ABRAMSON: Nancy?

NANCY: Yes?

MR ABRAMSON: Is that your name? Nancy?

NANCY: Yes.

MR ABRAMSON: Listen to me, Nancy. You have to hear this. I had a lover walk out on me fifty years ago. I was probably just a little older than you are now, and

I was devastated. Just recently, I found out that he left because of something he thought I'd done, which I hadn't done. And get this. He was with a friend of mine one night, just like we are now, and the friend urged him to call me. But he chickened out. And we both lost what may have been the love of our lives. Whenever you hit a crossroads in life of doing or not doing, do, because when you're old you'd rather say "What did I do?" than "What didn't I do?"

MARK: You never told me that.

MR ABRAMSON: (Covering the phone receiver) I'm making it up.

NANCY: We're all gonna ask him if he's gay?

MR ABRAMSON: Yes.

GENE: That's a mistake.

MARK: Yes what?

MR ABRAMSON: We're all gonna ask the boyfriend if he's gay.

MARK: So we are calling?

MR ABRAMSON: I think we've got a fighting chance!

GENE: Nancy, you do what you think is best. It's your life.

GRACE: But remember what Mister Abramson said.

NANCY: Oh call him. I don't care. It can't be worse.

MR ABRAMSON: (Squealing with glee to MARK) We're calling! We're calling!

MARK: I'm getting a nervous stomach.

MR ABRAMSON: Why? What do you care? He's not your boyfriend.

MARK: He could be.

GRACE: What's his number?

NANCY: Oh God.

GRACE: What's his number, Nancy?

GENE: Give her a second.

GRACE: What's his number?

NANCY: 521-3074.

GRACE: Hold on Donald. *(Dialing)* 5-2-1…

NANCY: 3074.

GRACE: …3-0-7-4

(BEN enters on his bed, wearing a robe, and carrying cookies and a glass of milk. His phone rings.)

BEN: Hello? *(Pause)* Hello?

NANCY: Hi Ben.

BEN: Hi Nance.

NANCY: How are you?

BEN: Okay.

NANCY: Did I wake you?

BEN: No. I can't sleep.

NANCY: Me neither.

BEN: I'm eating milk and cookies.

NANCY: What kind?

BEN: From the Phoenician bakery.

MR ABRAMSON: You mean the one on 9th Avenue?

BEN: Who said that?

MR ABRAMSON: *(Covering phone)* Oops.

NANCY: Uhh…

BEN: Are you alone?

NANCY: Not exactly.

BEN: Are you at home?

NANCY: No.

BEN: Are you on speaker-phone?

NANCY: Yes.

MARK: What's happening?

MR ABRAMSON: I shouldn't have said that.

MARK: Give me the phone!

BEN: Where are you?

NANCY: I'm at Grace's.

GRACE: Hi Ben.

NANCY: Grace is here.

GRACE: We thought Nancy needed some support.

BEN: Who asked about the bakery?

GRACE: Gene's here too. *(To GENE)* Say "hi".

GENE: Hi.

GRACE: Hi "Ben."

GENE: He knows who I mean. *(Leaning towards the phone)* I'm with you, brother.

BEN: What is going on?

NANCY: I wanted to ask you a question and I was talking to them about it, and I thought maybe it would be better if they were here, because you know how twisted we get when we're alone and it's late, so I thought, maybe with some objective people, we could stay straight, or...not crooked.

BEN: You told them about our fight?

NANCY: Yeah.

GRACE: We know all about it, Ben.

GENE: And I respect your right to privacy.

NANCY: I hope that's okay. Grace is my best friend. She's like family.

BEN: What about Gene?

NANCY: Gene's a hit—

(GENE *cuts her a look.*)

NANCY: I don't know so much about Gene.

BEN: People do have fights and deal with it themselves.

NANCY: I know.

GRACE: We just thought we might have some perspective on it.

MR ABRAMSON: I'm here too.

BEN: Who's that?

NANCY: Donald Abramson.

MR ABRAMSON: The Phoenician bakery is terrific. Usually when you say it, people think you're saying the Venetian bakery, because no one associates pastries with Phoenicians, who are thought of more as an ancient maritime culture.

BEN: Who is that?

NANCY: Donald Abramson.

BEN: Is he an historian?

NANCY: I don't think...well, maybe. (*To* MR ABRAMSON) Are you?

MR ABRAMSON: I'm in carpeting.

NANCY: He's not. He's a friend of Mark's.

BEN: Who's Mark?

GENE: He's my brother. I raised him since the sixth grade, when our mother, Bless Her Memory, passed away.

BEN: How many people do you have over there?

NANCY: They're not here.

BEN: They?

MR ABRAMSON: We're here.

NANCY: Mark too.

MR ABRAMSON: *(Quickly handing* MARK *the phone)* Say "hello."

MARK: *(Into the phone)* Hello.

GRACE: We have them on three-way calling, Ben.

BEN: So how many people are there?

GRACE: That's it. Just five.

BEN: And you all want to talk about our fight?

GENE: We're not all against you, Ben. I, for one, am very much for you.

GRACE: *(Hissing)* Gene!

MARK: I said calling you was a bad idea... *(Whispering to* MR ABRAMSON*)* What's his name?

MR ABRAMSON: How should I know? I can barely remember my own.

GRACE: Tell him, Nancy.

BEN: Tell me what?

GENE: She doesn't have to.

NANCY: Well, I felt...It's stupid.

BEN: What?

GRACE: Just say it.

GENE: Don't pressure her!

NANCY: This is a bad idea.

BEN: What?!

MARK: We're here for you, Nancy.

GENE: I'm here for Ben.

BEN: Who keeps saying that?

GRACE: Gene. The turn-coat. Tell him, Nancy.

BEN: Tell me what?

NANCY: Well…umm…you said something that made me feel weird.

BEN: When? What did I say?

NANCY: Tonight. You said…well…

BEN: What?

MR ABRAMSON: What's going on?

MARK: Just a second.

NANCY: You said you thought you might be gay.

BEN: What?!!

MARK: *(Covering phone, to* MR ABRAMSON*)* She said it!

MR ABRAMSON: What?

NANCY: You said sometimes you think you're gay.

MARK: *(Covering phone again)* The cat is out of the bag, and the boyfriend is out of the closet.

MR ABRAMSON: Yes!!!

BEN: I was making a point!

GRACE: Don't be defensive, Ben.

BEN: But she misunderstood what I said.

GENE: I had a feeling about this.

NANCY: I know you were making a point, but it came out of the blue.

BEN: It came out of my head. That's where points come from!

MARK: Give her a chance, Ben.

GRACE: He's getting aggressive.

GENE: Stick to your guns, Ben.

NANCY: It seemed to belie…

BEN: I am not gay!

GENE: Yeah! I knew it! *(Into phone)* I know you're not, Bennie!

MARK: Don't take sides, Gene. *(To* MR ABRAMSON*)* My brother is such a reactionary.

NANCY: But you said you've thought about it.

BEN: I have thought about it, but I've also thought about killing, and I'm not a murderer.

MARK: Murder and gay are not the same thing.

GENE: You can say that again.

GRACE: Murder and sex! Murder and sex!

MR ABRAMSON: Murder? What are you talking about, murder? Is that the hitman?

NANCY: You said you expected at some point to have an encounter.

BEN: Well maybe, but who knows?

MR ABRAMSON: Who was murdered?

MARK: No one.

MR ABRAMSON: I don't understand. Why murder?

NANCY: You seemed very open to it.

BEN: I'm an open guy.

GRACE: But how open, Ben?

BEN: I am not gay!

MARK: You say it like it's the plague!

BEN: I say it like it's what I'm not.

MARK: You say it defensively.

GENE: Stick to your guns, Ben!

BEN: Is that Gene?

GENE: Yeah.

BEN: Back off, Gene!

NANCY: *(Terrified)* Don't make him mad, Ben!

GRACE: *(To* GENE*)* Baby, he didn't mean it!

BEN: Who the hell is Gene?

GRACE: Mark's brother.

BEN: Who the hell is Mark?

GRACE: Gene's brother. And my therapist.

BEN: Jesus Christ, listen to me. I don't know any of you, and none of you know me, and I have nothing against gay people. It just so happens that many of my friends are…

MARK: …gay.

BEN: Yes, as a matter of fact. And anyway, I don't think people are gay or straight. I think they're just sexual.

GENE: Okay, you're losing me, Ben.

BEN: My point was that everything passes through us, and we're all those things.

NANCY: That was my point.

BEN: Well I agree with you. Now maybe in my intellectually hipster way I say I'm open to more than I am, but just because the idea of men has passed through me doesn't mean I'm gay.

MARK: *(To* MR ABRAMSON*)* He's straight.

NANCY: I felt very weird about it, like if you are gay, then who have I been sleeping with all these months.

BEN: But I'm not gay!

NANCY: But that's what I felt.

GRACE: She's just telling you what she felt, Ben.

BEN: Well I don't like five people sitting around telling me I'm gay when I'm not.

GENE: I agree.

MARK: *(To* MR ABRAMSON*)* He's not only straight. He's homophobic.

BEN: Who said that?

MR ABRAMSON: What did he say?

BEN: Who are you people to tell me what I am? And who are you, Nancy, to let them?

NANCY: I thought it would help.

BEN: Did you tell them what you are? Did you tell them what you called me?

GRACE: What did you call him?

NANCY: Nothing.

BEN: She didn't tell you?

NANCY: Come on, Ben.

MARK: What did you call him?

MR ABRAMSON: What did who call who?

MARK: *(To* MR ABRAMSON*)* Nancy called the boyfriend something.

MR ABRAMSON: Now?

MARK: No, before.

NANCY: I knew this was a bad idea.

GRACE: What did you call him?

BEN: You can call me gay, but you can't tell them you called me a hook-nosed Jew?

GRACE: *(Simultaneous)* A WHAT?!

MARK: *(Simultaneous)* WHAT?!

GENE: *(Simultaneous)* WHOA!

NANCY: I wish I were dead.

BEN: She called me a hook-nosed Jew in the middle of sex.

NANCY: At the end.

GRACE: You did?!

NANCY: It's none of your business—

BEN: But my being a flaming fag is?!

MARK: Now wait a second!

GRACE: Nancy, how could you say that?

MR ABRAMSON: What's going on?

MARK: You should be honored she thought you were gay.

BEN: It's emasculating.

MR ABRAMSON: What did she call him?

MARK: Then you have a fragile sense of masculinity, buster! Don't you call anyone a fag unless you are one.

BEN: Right! That's my point! She shouldn't call me a hook-nosed Jew unless she is one.

MARK: It's a good point.

GRACE: I can't believe you called him that.

MR ABRAMSON: What's a good point?

MARK: Nancy called Ben a hook-nosed Jew.

MR ABRAMSON: Oh my God! Give me the phone! *(Into the telephone)* Now listen here, little lady! I don't care if you're Jewish or not—

BEN: She's not.

MR ABRAMSON: Then that's appalling! People were killed with words like that. In my lifetime.

GRACE: *(To NANCY)* Why did you say it?

NANCY: Ohhhhh…

GENE: It's kind of messed up, Nancy. Even I know that.

BEN: She screamed it out when she was coming.

GRACE: You said it when you came?

BEN: Yeah! She screamed it!

MR ABRAMSON: Oh my goodness.

BEN: "Do me you hook-nosed Jew!"

GENE: Oh Madonna.

GRACE: Nancy.

MR ABRAMSON: You said that during sex? What kind of a crazy anti-Semite are you?

NANCY: I am not an anti-Semite!

GRACE: You're not making a very strong case for yourself.

NANCY: You don't understand what our sex is like.

MR ABRAMSON: The Gestapo?

NANCY: It's all out of context.

BEN: It was very disturbing.

NANCY: I explained it to you.

GENE: (To GRACE) You see what happens when you talk dirty.

MR ABRAMSON: And you had the gall to call us and say your boyfriend was queer?!

BEN: I'm straight!

NANCY: I didn't want to call anyone. I wanted to talk to Grace.

GRACE: Weren't you gonna tell me you called him a hook-nosed Jew?

MR ABRAMSON: Who said that?!

GRACE: I did.

GENE: Grace.

GRACE: But I was quoting Nancy.

MR ABRAMSON: I don't want to hear anyone say that anymore.

GRACE: Nancy, weren't you going to tell me?

BEN: Answer her, Nancy.

NANCY: No!

MARK: Put me on the phone.

MR ABRAMSON: No!

MARK: I want to ask her a question.

MR ABRAMSON: I'm not through with her.

MARK: Just for a second.

MR ABRAMSON: *(Into phone)* You listen to me, you Nancy...

BEN: I'm straight!

MR ABRAMSON: I meant the girl.

MARK: Would you gimme the phone! *(Grabs phone from MR ABRAMSON. Into phone)* Nancy. Are you there, Nancy?

NANCY: Yes.

MARK: When you said he stopped at the end, you didn't say you called him a hook-nosed Jew.

MR ABRAMSON: Jesus Fucking Christ!

MARK: I'm sorry, Mister Abramson. *(Back to NANCY)* You made it sound like a sex thing, not a racial vendetta.

MR ABRAMSON: Jews are not another race.

MARK: An ethnic vendetta.

BEN: You just barge in there, tell a bunch of people I'm gay, and omit the minor detail that you called me a hook-nosed Jew?! What the hell is that?

GRACE: Nancy, what are you thinking?

GENE: I have to say, Nancy, this casts you in a different light.

MARK: Nancy, I think you need professional counselling. I'd be happy to send you my card.

NANCY: I don't want your card!

MARK: I have a website.

BEN: Didn't you think it would come up in a party-line group-chat?!

MARK: www.gayshrink.com

GENE: *(To* NANCY*)* Maybe the problem isn't Ben, Nancy. Maybe it's you.

GRACE: Nancy, why don't you answer?

NANCY: I'm trying but everyone's talking so fast I can't even catch my breath.

GRACE: Don't avoid it Nancy.

MARK: And don't lash out.

GENE: Alright, give her some air.

NANCY: I'm not avoiding anything.

GENE: But you still have to tell us.

GRACE: When did you become in charge?

GENE: She still has to tell us, but we have to give her some air.

MR ABRAMSON: What's she saying?

MARK: She says she's not avoiding.

BEN: Then speak.

NANCY: I'm speaking.

GRACE: Nancy, why did you say it?

NANCY: I don't know, okay?! I don't know! Don't you ever say things and you don't know why?

GRACE: Nothing like that.

NANCY: Don't things slip when you're not thinking sometimes, because you're feeling?!

MARK: Yes.

MR ABRAMSON: Yes what?

MARK: She's feeling.

NANCY: Your body is feeling! Or your soul?!

MARK: Her soul is feeling.

BEN: *(Simultaneous with* MR ABRAMSON*)* Your soul called me a hook-nosed Jew?

MR ABRAMSON: *(Simultaneous with* BEN*)* Her soul called him a hook-nosed Jew?

NANCY: No! Sometimes you're with someone and you want to say something you're not allowed to say, because for one second you're relaxed enough to say it, not because you mean it, but just because you say it, because you're alone with someone who knows you. You can be a bad person for one second. You're the one who said that, Ben, that the whole point of being in love was that you don't have to explain yourself.

BEN: Yeah, but…

MR ABRAMSON: What's happening now?

GENE: That's wrong, Nancy. Sometimes you do have to explain yourself. That's what I'm telling Grace.

BEN: Is that Gene? He's right. Listen to Gene.

GENE: *(To* GRACE*)* You see?

MARK: You're not addressing the core, Nancy.

BEN: Some things you do have to explain.

GRACE: *(To* GENE*)* I cannot believe he's quoting you.

GENE: That's what I been tellin' you, Grace.

GRACE: What?

GENE: I got it goin' on.

MR ABRAMSON: What's happening?!

MARK: It's not about freedom, Nancy.

MR ABRAMSON: What's about freedom?

NANCY: Yes it is!

MARK: No it isn't.

GENE: What's it about, Mark?

BEN: That's what I'd like to know.

NANCY: It's about sex! It's about joining together! And your Jewish thing is different! Okay?! It's just different!

MARK: Now we're getting somewhere.

MR ABRAMSON: Where? Where are we getting?

BEN: I know it's different.

NANCY: And when you're in me, I want it to be the same. I want to get rid of the differences!

GRACE: But if you're saying he's gay, you're making differences.

MARK: *(Gently, persistently to* NANCY*)* What about the Jewish thing?

MR ABRAMSON: What Jewish thing?

NANCY: *(Crying out)* It excludes me!

MARK: There you are.

MR ABRAMSON: Where? Where are we?

NANCY: *(Crying)* I feel like you're gonna break up with me, because I'm not Jewish!

MARK: That's it. *(To* MR ABRAMSON*)* They got it.

MR ABRAMSON: What? What did they get?

GENE: *(Marvelling)* Ohh, I see. It's the Jewish thing.

MARK: Fear.

MR ABRAMSON: It's always the fear.

NANCY: *(Crying)* You do those Jewish things, and you never talk about it, and you never share it…

GENE: Grace, if you'd just share.

GRACE: Gene! I have known you for five days!

NANCY: …and maybe you'll want that more.

BEN: Nancy…

NANCY: *(Crying)* And I wanted to reject you before you rejected me!

MARK: That's it.

MR ABRAMSON: What is going on?

BEN: But Nancy, there's always differences.

GENE: Yeah, right. You see, Grace? There's always differences. You gotta share the differences.

GRACE: He is her boyfriend! You are my boy-toy!

MARK: They found the key.

NANCY: *(Crying)* But I don't want you to break up with me…

GENE: No one's breaking up with anybody. Don't break up with her, Ben. Grace, give me a chance.

GRACE: You are not my boyfriend!!

GENE: We really gotta talk.

NANCY: *(Crying)* And I'm…scared…

MARK: Aww, you see? *(To MR ABRAMSON)* Nancy's scared Ben'll break up with her.

MR ABRAMSON: So she called him a— Oi yoi yoi.

MARK: It's complicated.

BEN: Nancy...

NANCY: *(Crying)* What?

BEN: You should come back.

GENE, GRACE, MARK, & NANCY: Aww...

MR ABRAMSON: What?

GENE: That's nice, Ben. Go to him, Nancy.

GRACE: He's right. Go to him.

NANCY: *(Crying)* I'm afraid.

BEN: You don't have to be afraid.

GENE: Don't be afraid.

MARK: Go, Nancy. *(Putting phone to* MR ABRAMSON's *mouth)* Say "go".

MR ABRAMSON: Go. *(To* MARK*)* Why did I say that? Where's she going?

NANCY: *(Crying)* I don't want you to break up with me.

BEN: I won't. We'll just talk and figure it out.

GENE: *(To* GRACE*)* I think we could figure it out.

GRACE: Gene, have I done something to confuse you?

MARK: *(To* MR ABRAMSON*)* Ben wants her back.

MR ABRAMSON: I wouldn't take her back, the racist pig.

NANCY: The whole point of coming to this city was that Grace said I would meet someone like you, and before you sat by me in the library, and told me about your books and your poetry, I didn't see how I was ever going to meet anybody. And maybe because you never sweet-talked me, I haven't been sure when it would stop.

BEN: No one ever knows for sure, Nancy. We're all just wanderers.

MARK: *(To* MR ABRAMSON*)* He's nice.

MR ABRAMSON: He's a wimp. What did he say?

MARK: We're all wanderers.

MR ABRAMSON: Only a Jew would say that.

GRACE: Just go to him, Nancy.

NANCY: Well...

GENE: She's right, Nancy. Go to him.

NANCY: I feel...

MARK: Nancy, if you don't go now, you'll never go.

BEN: It'll be okay, Nancy.

GRACE: Please, Nancy. Go.

GENE: It's the right decision.

MR ABRAMSON: That kid is askin' for trouble.

NANCY: *(Quietly)* Okay. Okay. *(With* GRACE*'s help,* NANCY *readies herself)* Okay.

*(*GENE *and* GRACE *help* NANCY *exit.)*

NANCY: *(Continues muttering)* Okay.

GRACE: *(Offstage)* Bye, Nancy.

GENE: *(Offstage)* Bye.

BEN: Are you coming? Nancy? You gotta come. Listen. I know I'm not a big complimenter, and maybe I don't tell you like I should how great you are and beautiful, but part of the reason is because I hear guys tell you that all the time, you know?

*(*GENE *and* GRACE *return.)*

BEN: We walk down the street, and they say it. We get on a bus, and the bus driver says it. My friends say it right after they meet you. And I don't want to sound like all of them, because for me how you look and who you are is all wrapped up together in your face and your body and your mind, and how free and open and funny and smart and sexy you are. You know? You're like this crazy loose cannon that sends me reeling. And I want to be on the inside of all that, where your beauty is such a part of me, I'd have to step out of my own skin to say it. Nancy? *(Pause)* Nancy?

GENE: *(Imitating* NANCY's *voice)* Yes?

BEN: You. Are. Beautiful. *(Pause)* Nancy?

GRACE: She just ran right out the door, Ben. You can hang up. You did a lovely job.

MARK: You did beautifully.

GENE: Good work, Bennie.

BEN: Thank you all. For your help.

GENE: *(Starting to cry)* You did it yourself, kid. And we all learned something. Even Grace.

MARK: You deserve it, Ben.

MR ABRAMSON: Deserve what?

BEN: I'm sorry if I...

MARK: Don't you dare apologize.

GRACE: Just get ready for her, Ben.

GENE: Yeah, Ben. Be real nice.

MARK: That's right.

BEN: Okay.

GENE: Good luck, Ben. Way to go.

BEN: Thanks. Bye.

GRACE & MARK: Bye

(BEN *hangs up.)*

MARK: *(To* GENE*)* I'll talk to you in a second.

MARK: *(To* MR ABRAMSON.*)* She's going back.

GRACE: Mark?

MR ABRAMSON: Can we get off the phone now?

MARK: It's sweet. That was great, Grace.

GRACE: You were wonderful, Mark. Thank you.

GENE: We did real good.

GRACE: You didn't even want to call.

GENE: I know. I was wrong.

GRACE: Mark, do you think they'll stay together?

MARK: No.

GRACE: Neither do I.

GENE: They might.

MR ABRAMSON: What?

MARK: They won't stay together.

MR ABRAMSON: Like Hitler and Golda Meir.

GRACE: We're gonna go, Mark. Thank Donald for us.

MARK: I will. And Grace, give Gene a chance. There's more there than you think.

GRACE: It's just sex.

MARK: Give him a chance anyway. I owe him everything. Goodnight, Gene.

GENE: Goodnight little brother.

MR ABRAMSON: Can we go to sleep now?

MARK: Sleep? Where were we?

MR ABRAMSON: I'm too tired for that.

MARK: No you're not.

MR ABRAMSON: Maybe tomorrow.

MARK: We'll see about that.

GENE: I do think you could like me for more than just sex, Grace.

GRACE: We'll talk about it in the morning.

GENE: *(As they crawl into bed)* I mean, I gotta lotta good instincts with people, a lotta good qualities. I'm a good listener, a good talker, I bake bread, I'm nice with children...

(GRACE's curled up)

GENE: And I think I could fill you up with something you don't have.

(GRACE's hand touches GENE's face. NANCY enters from upstage-center and sits on BEN's bed.)

BEN: Hi.

NANCY: Hi.

BEN: How are you doing?

NANCY: Okay.

BEN: It's been quite a night.

NANCY: Yeah.

BEN: I'm glad you came back.

NANCY: Really? You don't think I'm vanilla?

BEN: No.

NANCY: Or anti-Semitic?

BEN: No.

NANCY: And you're not gay?

BEN: No.

(Pause. They begin to take off their clothes. BEN helps NANCY with her shirt.)

NANCY: I'm sleepy.

BEN: We'll have a deep sleep

(They crawl into bed.)

MR ABRAMSON: I don't know if I can.

MARK: Just enjoy it.

GRACE: *(Happily surprised)* Gene! You're a little wound up.

GENE: Yeah.

MR ABRAMSON: I'm too old.

MARK: You're just right.

GRACE: Oh, Gene.

GENE: Yeah. I'm a little "stimulated".

GRACE: Talk to me baby.

GENE: Uhh…I'm a little "stimulated".

GRACE: Talk to me.

MR ABRAMSON: Maybe tomorrow.

MARK: Just feel it.

GENE: Grace?

GRACE: Yes?

GENE: I'm gonna…get you.

GRACE: Oh you are, Clean Gene?

MR ABRAMSON: *(Suprised)* That feels nice.

MARK: You feel nice.

MR ABRAMSON: That feels good.

MARK: You're good.

GRACE: Give it to me, Gene.

GENE: I'm gonna give it to you.

GRACE: Give it to me.

GENE: I'm GONNA give it to you.

MR ABRAMSON: Something is happening.

MARK: You know what's happening.

GRACE: Talk dirty to me Gene!

GENE: I'm gonna get you!

GRACE: Talk dirty to me.

GENE: I'm getting you?

MR ABRAMSON: Maybe I can, Mark!

MARK: You're a fountain of youth.

GRACE: Fuck me Gene!

GENE: I'm...fuckin' you!

MR ABRAMSON: I think I can!

MARK: You know you can!

MR ABRAMSON: I think I can!

MARK: You know you can!

GENE: I'm fucking you!

GRACE: Fuck me!

MR ABRAMSON: I think I can!

GENE: I'm fucking you!

GRACE: Fuck me!

MARK: You know you can.

GENE: I'm fucking you!

GRACE: Fuck me!

MR ABRAMSON: I think I can!

GENE: I'm fucking you!

MARK: You know you can!

GRACE: Fuck me!

MR ABRAMSON: I THINK I CAN!!!!!

MARK: YOU KNOW YOU CAN, YOU HOOK-NOSED JEW!!!!!!!

GENE: I'M FUCKING YOU, YOU SELFISH, STUCK-UP, NYMPHO, BITCH DYKE!!!!!!!

(Pause)

GRACE & MR ABRAMSON: What?

(Blackout)

END OF PLAY

CPSIA information can be obtained
at www.ICGtesting.com
Printed in the USA
LVHW041003210120
644246LV00017B/719

9 780881 456110